ECLIPSE

Books by Natalie Robins

Wild Lace
My Father Spoke of His Riches
The Peas Belong on the Eye Level
Eclipse

ECLIPSE

Natalie Robins

Swallow Press
Ohio University Press
Chicago   Athens, Ohio   London

Swallow Press Books
are published by
Ohio University Press
Athens, Ohio

Library of Congress Cataloging in Publication Data

Robins, Natalie S.
  Eclipse.

  I. Title.
PS3535.02165E4   811'.54   80-28680
ISBN 0-8040-0367-X
ISBN 0-8040-0368-8 (pbk.)

Some of these poems originally appeared in *The Bellevue Press
Poetry Post Card Series, Connections, The Humanist, The Nation,
Open Places, Poetry, Tri-Quarterly Review, The Village Voice.*

for Christopher
for Rachel
for Noah

CONTENTS

PART ONE

Returning

Memorial

for my father

June
arrives
over the mountain's
shrill fall.
June arrives
on green sticks;
branches hide
burial grounds.

Abandoned Boat

Holding out for richer anchors, the boat floats
across the bay, no exits in sight, no stopping
to say the day is longer than any of its used
parts, no narrowing down into spilling circles,
no leaving behind spent waves.

Onboard, a broken anchor, used last week,
and fixed to spare sailing through the air:
no hands will hold it now, pull it from
its locker on the planks, no eyes will say
it's there to stop the boat from pushing out
to sea.

Run by no one, left behind, no food, no light,
no drink: the boat is waiting for a better way.
The paint, chipped and dull, runs out to waves
it cannot use.

Challah

for Blu and Irving Greenberg

Sabbath bread dreams of childhood,
the nightmares dance in ovens.

(Why isn't bawrooch ahtaw adonoi
spilling out of these eyes?)

Sabbath bread rises,
then circles in prayer—
or is it a kiss before birth?

(Why isn't ellohaynoo melech haw-olawm
breaking famine on these breasts?)

Sabbath bread mixes with wine;
one holy meal was finished
thirty years ago.

(Why isn't sheh-heh-cheh-yawnoo
v'keey'mawnoo
stained on these fingers?)

Sabbath bread bursts into law:
the screams
(or scars)
remain as hymns.

(Why isn't v'heegee awnoo
laz'mahn hah-zeh
running through these legs?)

Sabbath bread falls and sends us home
where gestures
bend our lips to silver
and love surrounds the
rescued word:
Amen.

5

Uncle Nachman's Funeral

Death opens up like a flower
certain faces whose lives
have been marked I AM DEAD
TO YOU.
Cousins, now grown and real,
ask: who are you?

Nachman rocks the earth,
stones fly up, uncovering
gestures never before used.

"He had a real lust for life
and living . . . his friends
were both Jewish and non-Jewish . . .

During these last years he lived
near the Surfside Nursing Home.
He even made an arc for them . . ."

A face turns out perfectly true
words and there is a lie
over Nachman's coffin.

"Enlightened citizen . . . who helped
the Flatbush Police Department . . .
Nathan was truly a simple man . . .
for people as beautiful . . . the
imperishable crown of a good name . . ."

How can the truth be seen along
the busy street of one tone?

Bored Rabbi,
"as a direct outgrowth
of his love for Judaism . . ."
Nachman suffers your inexact voice
as his last sound
before the earth praises
his own fine rhythms.

Dead uncle, I loved your face.
Is it grinning
at the inappropriate
fierce tone that sends it home?

At the graveyard,
crowded as a cattle car,
there is talk of cost
before they plunge your body
back to earth.

The American-flagged and blue-jeaned
servant of the yard, arms black
from sweat or sour dirt,
spits
before you fall.
His aim is not as perfect as your son's,
who packs rich soil on your eyes.

You watched them both
and asked that spit be spared your space
until the family leaves.
The soil folds in wide,
caressing your new frame
with insistence, joy, and speed.

Dead uncle, I loved your face.
Is it watching mine?

One tear fell
as you went down below my sights,
it wasn't meant for you—
but fell for all the others,
dead with good words, or with bad.

Changes

"My mother said
come here.
She had no body on,
only her head walking on hair."
Wide beliefs
are not full of bone she knows,
the stairs are no longer firm—
am I climbing back or are you falling?
My father holds her arms around his neck,
the legs trail across the landing.
Mother, mother
pull at air:
now your life is inside mine.

(The quoted lines are from a poem by Mary Cheever and are used with the poet's permission.)

For Eleven New Priests

"God here now as Father and judge sees you trying to make stones into bread. You can only offer up the smell and sound and sight of perversion."
     —Reverend George W. Rutler of Rosemont, Pa., at the Church of the Advocate in North Philadelphia, Pa. as eleven women were ordained as Episcopal priests.

You are not my father and never will be,
my bread sinks into my own mouth, too;
it rises with each breath I discover
near my heart—
this organ pumps life into me,
it is not a stone anymore.

I lie,
Reverend Rutler;
my heart is now a stone
which I offer to you
as a treasure, even as a fine jewel.

It comes from me, Reverend Rutler,
a woman's heart of stone
comes from me,
and when this jewel isn't offered to you,
it can be seen daily and nightly
in a soft, safe place
where it beats secrets
to my husband
and daughter,
my doctors and mothers,
my brothers
and a very few friends.

Reverend Rutler, I smell like a woman.
The odors from my body come from my poems
from my play about a man having a baby
from my children's book about death
from my novel about crime
from my neighbors

from my shopping trips on Riverdale Avenue
from my friends
from the children I teach to write poems
from my family
from all my acts of love.

Reverend Rutler,
I sound like a woman, too.
I speak of goodness and energy
and dying and loving.
I speak of politics and boot polish.
Sometimes I touch instead of speaking,
sometimes I speak and touch:
Reverend Rutler, don't I see you?

My god is not the same as yours,
in truth I have no god at all.
But here's what you seem to say:
    Who invented you?   God.
    Who invented me?   You.

How come I am not me in the eyes of your god?

Something in your eyes
says you are going to accept my gift.
Have you forgotten
I've offered up my heart of stone?

It will come slowly at first,
then it will seem just right.
The temperature
will be ideal for anything full-bodied,
even any mouths that might be ready
to bite down hard
on one word: Rock.

Reverend Rutler,
wasn't the ride to North Philadelphia
full of all kinds of thirst?
One kind?

The gift, if you accept it,
gets easier and easier to swallow.

It is not soft or grainy
or vitamin-enriched.
The gift, Reverend Rutler,
gets easier and easier
to produce,
gets easier and easier
to bake
            high
            or
            low

as long as you remove yourself,
stay away from
my
warm
inviting
oven.

Poem For Rachel's Fourth Birthday

Let us go
across the yard together,
letting go of twigs and stones:
a clearing out for winter space.

I drop a hand along the way,
you hardly notice
as you rush toward one hundred and sixty fingers
moving leaves into story books.

I need you close,
but let you grow closer to yourself.

See me keep the night from freezing
in November wind?

Put your open eyes on my face,
I move closed lips on your words.
Will we see reunion in the morning
as the sun pours climbing light?

Thinking About My Mother's Death on her Sixty-Eighth Birthday

The open skies
offer nothing new
to my bulging eyes,
what can rain create
except thicker leaves
or taller grass?

December shed everything,
nothing much is left for
January or February to swallow whole.
Snow will be the color
of the sheets
wrapped across a dying body.

But no one's death has been announced.
It's her birthday.
Nothing's changed.

The rain covers everything
with a clear disguise:
I notice seeds that are now dark
and moist.
Will they spring up in someone else's garden?
Will I have to shut my eyes?

Returning

His stares
polish words that come and go
or stay to press light.
I could conceivably die for him,
and why?
I don't know where his hand goes
after it leaves mine!
I can't hear him listen to words that aren't mine.

It must be linked to some dream of worlds that splinter
not at all,
worlds that sit rigidly on blocks of nightmare.

It's hard to return here
after such a long and peaceful absence—
but children have the habit of reminding us
where we've been,
while older faces
carry seams that fall together
in a wholly practical way:
is function less than meets my eye?

A giant sea turtle
climbs into this head at night
and my skin accepts its shell as kin.

Returning, going back, walking in and returning—
to him
who quietly discovers why legends hurt
and what use they have before they're done with us
or why they come and go like bats.

I hear nothing around me.
Bees
or crickets—
these are noises inside my arms.

I see nothing at all.
At eleven o'clock the lights are gone,
the house is empty—

my legs run away from hundreds of portraits.

I understand nothing at all.
My questions confuse all the answers.
I am not real.
I have no bones
that crack or spill across wide floors.

I am dying here alone.
I am dying into many pieces.
Soon
I will be a web of threads
made light by sun.

Soon
I will be carried high by a breeze.
Soon
I will settle in earth
and grow strong.

PART TWO

Seasons and Trees

Autumn Snow/ And War Is Still Falling

An early winter target
is hit with morning
like a circling bullet;
top-a-rap-a-top-a-rap-a-
        bing,
off twelve o'clock thermometers.

Sun, then snow, in quick rounds
drops transparently to the ground.
What about our harvest
of gold and shocking indoor flowers?
Impatiens gone to seed,
an irregular grave in sight
underground.

We watch autumn
flattened like a bomb.
Crashing though the air,
pellets of iron mist
land on their targets:
top-a-rap-a-top-a-rap-a-
        bing,
off human error.

Eclipse

For I. Herbert Scheinberg

I.

I remember seeing the thick black thighs of darkness
move as rhythmically as a beam of clear sunlight
caught in early morning wind . . .
After the first eclipse, the others
seem to hide much more:
and so begins
an
open circle that trails each new
fully negotiable
eclipse
of the sun. Everytime it happens,
everytime a cover slaps hard and brilliantly,
it's happening only once.
It's happening one time, but once again, a repetition
of the earth's moves;
and the earth's shape
keeps mine
my eclipse   the eclipse of my ribs
intact.
I hide inside myself. I cover up
more than is framed by bone.

II.

The African rocks absorbed no sweat,
fast winds pushed my arms to my face, my
hands to my eyes: it's June 30, 1973, and
the *Saros 6* eclipse of our solar planet has
occurred. I notice the
thick black thighs
of our guide as Omary returns us to camp.
The thighs
can dance their directions
but I am still looking in the sky.

III.

I remember night kisses sucking out day light, even hot
sunlight . . .
After the first eclipse, the others
protect with more daring, the others withhold
space
so that space holds less of *other* light.
I remember night kisses sucking out dark clouds, dark
whispers . . .

IV.

Wild animals surround our camp, we
are safe
inside
the stone and water tents of *Loiengalani.*
Inside
we hide our eyes, we hide
more than our eyes now that we are home.
We shut our eyes
alone
with nothing else to remember to hide
after
night kisses our sun expedition out of range.

V.

I remember seeing the thick black thighs of darkness
move as rhythmically as a beam of clear sunlight
caught in early morning wind . . .

School Pieces

The hardening across the yard
reaches far into the children's faces,
there is a sense of frozen speech
moving past the nursery songs
that see-saw out of doors
in the wind
by the window.
Time settles very quickly
into a pattern of do this do that
do the other thing last do the right thing
do it wrong do it over and over again
in no time at all.

Snow falls flat on our faces,
lace chapters open up into
a special category
of the season's cool, talkative
elegance.
Children walk into ice paintings,
snow on their teeth marks their limits,
ice is oddly comforting today.

*

What if hands were wooden,
feet or ears the same?
Everything as the yellow animals,
straight as sticks,
no blood to bend,
no muscle to feed
into the shape of her.

*

Wheels
as rectangular ideas to pound
into recognizable shapes
round the language
round the speech of small children
spinning old words and new words.
Oh yes
Oh no
around the mouths of perfectly
symmetrical truths.

*

Beat, beat
the heart ticks off the alphabet.
Falling across the floor
a handful of z's or b's or q's or u's,
the broom appears
and mirrors the letters of the body.

Hanging in the afternoon air,
salted, honestly,
peppered, accurately,
one T,
an irridescent snake S,
a sweet B:
language swallowed whole.

*

The story concerns a small delicate rabbit
moving up a big mountain,
the small delicate rabbit climbs slowly,
reaches a corner where snow has been for years,
the snow is white as snow,
the rabbit, small and delicate,
is snow and white.
The rabbit,
snow and white and small and delicate
is perfectly lost against the snow.
Where is rabbit now?
Find her.

Rivers, rivers,
a truck crossing into finger rivers,
a bridge of lines,
good x's, too,
that understand tunnels as well.

*

Mother is holding on to her name.
The same, thirty years ago,
thirty years ago!
It's like *tomorrow*.
There's talk of leaving behind.
What?
Nothing stays in place.

Tricks

Trick #1

Fasten two thumbs
to one spring flowered collar,
surround the body with seeing eye bulbs
that come up straight to the heart.
Let go
because the thumbs are weary.

Trick #2

Ask for a vocabulary of similes:
you are simple like a bowl of grapes,
you are warm like a pale white lamb,
you are wise like a gold and slippery knife.
Use the knife to halve the grapes,
butcher the lamb in silence.

Trick #3

Hold out both arms.
Watch for strangers.
Embrace and know:
stay inside and see
how knowledge holds its breath.

Trick #4

Rehearse.

Winter Tears

Under cold wood
I wear hot sun
which chokes me.

Do I cry
because
I am still shivering?

Are the tears
because
the heat
finally gets under something
and doesn't forget me?
Hasn't forgotten me?

Cold holds still,
waiting
to return under barren trees.

Shadow

Sun: following my shadow,
you are lost this afternoon.
The day opens up
and you sink like an anchor.
You've changed your ways.
The darkness,
will we see around it clearly?
Bend our eyes to watch deep circles?
Sun: we run from you.
Will you twist around and fall?
I won't catch you.
The moon,
shadows even,
has wrapped its light around my waist.

Winter Peace

Peace sits so still.
At the bottom of the hill,
the sleds are stopped by grass.

Waiting For Rain

There's this strong wind presentation.
It comes up across the center of the noon
and acts alone,
pulling down half-waxed leaves
and dead sticks,
dead as broken windows.

The rock speaks:
"I'm suffering here,
having been tossed roughly across the yellow lawn,
landing on,
or better still,
breaking into,
a flat, dusty, rectangular piece of glass.
Oh lord."

The window speaks:
"I'm an unusual view,
a center space overlooking falling, skinny shapes of landscape.
It was a lavender invader,
or creamy-green, at least,
that entered most intimately,
tearing clear features into glass stars. Oh yes."

There's this strong wind presentation.
It comes up across the center of the noon
and acts alone,
pulling down whole blossoms and live buds,
as alive as woman humming day songs.

The poet speaks:
"I'm suffering here,
having been tossed roughly across the borders of my house,
landing on,
or better still,
breaking into
an echo of madness.
What is to be saved?"

The poem speaks:
"I'm an unusual view,
a center space overlooking falling, skinny shapes of landscape.
It was an invasion of good will that lost its name, or shame,
abandoned its unsteady course
and tore at flesh:
my own!
The poet's trust is handled by the wind,
blowing
blowing
high into the clouds
to wait for rain. Oh yes."

Seasons and Trees

This I know
from the world,
that
if you take a tree across
some
hard words like I am not going with you,
sooner or later branches will stick to clouds
like
colors on a map, any map.
Or,
if you take wind and try to watch it float
over your palms,
some season will take issue
and
become too tired to change
from what it was
to what is must become.
Or,
if you take someone's hand
and feel it pull away,
you
must
not run or chase or follow.
Hands that
can blow about like fallen leaves
are
not like mine,
this I know.

PART THREE

Birth Elegy

Birth Elegy I

Winter hopes
simply die, more than once—
not more than is bearable,
but too quickly,
so quickly
the reason for any season at all
disappears.
It is here
dead skin grows seeds
and such a sight is worse than
any sudden death, but is sudden death
itself,
is the end of all snows,
is a lone empty tree
stretching dry branches high, high
toward grief.

Birth Elegy II

Baby daughter I'll never
know, I'll never see, I'll
never feel: I love you.

Birth Elegy III

Why does rope bind us?
Are there other uses?

Birth Elegy IV

It was a warm but winter Thursday,
quiet, full of time spent
hearing heart beats.
Hers was lost.
Someone cried we'll find it:
a deep incision, strong tugs
until she, herself, was seen,
eyes closed, mouth down,
arms and legs as silent
as her mother's voice.
Around her neck, the line
that brought her life and
brought her death.

Birth Elegy V

Across the hall, a stout woman
calls out: take my baby, take
my baby, I'm much too nervous
to feed him tonight.
I listen.

Birth Elegy VI

I've learned something:
nothing is fair, but
you can't change the rules.

Birth Elegy VII

One week and one day, her shadow
clings to mine: is she as beautiful
as all silhouettes?
Would she have stayed close or
would she have chosen to stray into
open sunlight?
I can see her fingers play
with the lace patterns
early morning rays strike on
the stark black floor of the
hospital corridor.

Birth Elegy VIII

Dear one, how can I miss you so
much when I have no sight on
your eyes? I have no sound from
your throat, I have no feel of
your thighs, I have nothing
of yours except your absence.

Birth Elegy IX

Under some protruding rock,
somewhere, even in the sky
I suppose,
there has to be a reason for
innocence choking on human error.

Birth Elegy X

Please, I ask myself this
question, no one else has to listen,
but where, where in all the spaces
of wind that whip across our faces
is it written that some remain empty
forever?

Birth Elegy XI

I worry about next December
second, and the one after that,
and all that will follow her
for the rest of my loss.

Birth Elegy XII

The fog closes in around tall
buildings, a cement truck throws
off its fill to a fourth floor
window of building H.
What is being covered up
or what is being born up there?
Why go to all that trouble
to bring hardness to a single
small window four stories
off the ground?

Birth Elegy XIII

She's crying now, only she
doesn't belong to me. No, I
haven't gone off the deep end.
She's my neighbor's baby girl,
swaddled in a yellow hospital
cover, lying inside a clear
plastic space capsule
that sends signals directly to me.

Birth Elegy XIV

Naomi spoke to me this morning:
"I told the tall black nurse
to tell you I've been where
you are now. Naomi, my mother
said to me, God will fill your
arms again. I'll never take
anything for granted again.
I look at my new boy's arms
rise up to me and I cry out,
blessed earth you have brought
me back and I'll follow you
now into any place at all."

Birth Elegy XV

Patience told me: "I'm scared,
but I can see you are, too."
Yes,
I'm scared of plotting new moves,
while you are scared
of moving the plot presented to you
last Saturday as Jason Charles. (I
heard your husband say his name.)

Birth Elegy XVI

There's nothing left after
grief leaves: except the waves
that remind us where we've been
and why we left
and how we can follow
grieving to its source:
beginning again.

Birth Elegy XVII

I can go into her room
and scream at the empty walls
and pound at the empty crib,
but the sound of my scream
is too silent
to be heard outside the room—
and the pounding of my fists
in the moist air
is too loud to be believed
inside the room.

Birth Elegy XVIII

The house holds her silence
like a rain cloud.
What will burst open?

Birth Elegy XIX

The attic now carries twelve
green plastic bags: her things,
wrapped in the color of
growing things—
plants and vines
that respond to care,
flowers and vegetables
that bloom all year long.

Birth Elegy XX

Some people have tried to say
you've got to forget her existence.
Why?
Why forget what I carried for nine
strong months?
She lived for an instant.
Isn't that more than some of us
ever become?

Birth Elegy XXI

Why should I have to listen to dead
people talk about how to handle
death?
Death is for the living.

Birth Elegy XXII

Rachel asked, "But, Mommy,
how did the cord tighten
if no one was at the other
end to pull it?"

Birth Elegy XXIII

Thirteen days ago, while I was asleep,
for a brief moment I had
two daughters.
Rachel and Rebekka.
Rebekka: gone now, gone before
we met, gone before our eyes could
mesh, gone before I awoke.

Birth Elegy XXIV

The tears
fall out of me
at the oddest times: when
I'm ready to fall asleep
at night,
when I wake up fresh
in the early morning,
when I look down at the dark,
clean floor boards,
when I watch two stray black cats
keep their distance
on the steps
in front of my house,
when I water the plants,
when I discover a song
easing its way past my whispers.

Birth Elegy XXV

Rebekka, you would have
loved it here with us.
We miss you.
Did you have my brown eyes?
Did you have your father's sandy
hair?
Was my father's grin on your lips?
Would you have grown up thin?
Would you have been kind?
Oh, sweet Rebekka, why did
you leave us so soon?
You would have loved it here
with us.

Birth Elegy XXVI

Next summer, when the hot
sand fits my feet like flesh,
when the cool water fits my face
like a Halloween mask, there'll be
three of us watching the ocean
stretch and stretch into a universe
of shells and rocks, there'll be
three of us learning that the waves
come and go, come and go, bringing
new colors, new rhythms, new lives.

Birth Elegy XXVII

Fifteen days.
The scar on my belly
is dry and empty.
The surgical medicine still stains
the spot where my belly was once
round and full of life.
The scar,
the one sitting on the edge
of my fingers, on the corners
of my eyes, on the sides of my brain,
that one is moist and full:
it will soon grow eyes that
will be able to see into the past:
was she beautiful?

Birth Elegy XXVIII

Someone sends a Christmas card.
Joy To The Four Of You.
But why not?
We *were* four, are three again,
but shouldn't she have joy, too?
I'll call and tell Willy
the baby is dead.
Will he want to remove the joy
from his card or will he still
wish joy to the four of us,
when there were four, briefly,
for a few minutes, fifteen days
ago, twenty three before Christmas
day.

Birth Elegy XXIX

Happy New Year, Rebekka.
We wish you could see how
much space there is in the house
now that you are gone.
There is more space
than was here
before you came.
Your death has moved things
aside, spread out our places,
put our bodies in corners
not spoken of before.
Rebekka, I don't want to have
this much room anymore.

Birth Elegy XXX

She travels everywhere we do.
She goes high in the air
at times, too, goes far
underground
and sometimes stays in one place.
She is inside me again,
a steady form that tells *us*
secrets:
she can move around—unseen by
others, she can speak with silent
verbs.
Rebekka, Rebekka, why did you die?